YOUR KNOWLEDGE HAS VALUE

- We will publish your bachelor's and master's thesis, essays and papers

- Your own eBook and book - sold worldwide in all relevant shops

- Earn money with each sale

Upload your text at www.GRIN.com
and publish for free

Bibliographic information published by the German National Library:

The German National Library lists this publication in the National Bibliography; detailed bibliographic data are available on the Internet at http://dnb.dnb.de .

This book is copyright material and must not be copied, reproduced, transferred, distributed, leased, licensed or publicly performed or used in any way except as specifically permitted in writing by the publishers, as allowed under the terms and conditions under which it was purchased or as strictly permitted by applicable copyright law. Any unauthorized distribution or use of this text may be a direct infringement of the author s and publisher s rights and those responsible may be liable in law accordingly.

Imprint:

Copyright © 2017 GRIN Verlag
Print and binding: Books on Demand GmbH, Norderstedt Germany
ISBN: 9783668656383

This book at GRIN:

https://www.grin.com/document/414663

Benaiah Mayabi

Human Population in the Future

GRIN Verlag

GRIN - Your knowledge has value

Since its foundation in 1998, GRIN has specialized in publishing academic texts by students, college teachers and other academics as e-book and printed book. The website www.grin.com is an ideal platform for presenting term papers, final papers, scientific essays, dissertations and specialist books.

Visit us on the internet:

http://www.grin.com/

http://www.facebook.com/grincom

http://www.twitter.com/grin_com

Running head: HUMAN POPULATION

Human Population

By Benaiah Mayabi

HUMAN POPULATION

Currently, there is more human population than the available natural resources to sustain such rising numbers of people (Mittal & Mittal, 2013). The highest rates of population increase are in the developing countries which are also characterized by poverty among other social problems. It follows therefore that these countries need to move with speed to tame and regulate the surging populations because failure to do so may mean less or no survival in the few coming years. Third world countries need to come up with policies to regulate population as this would be the only way out of the problem we could be heading into because of large populations and less resources to sustain such populations (Mittal & Mittal, 2013). It is evident that while world populations keep on increasing, the natural resources we depend on keep on reducing which means that there is too much pressure on the environment to provide what it cannot. Biodiversity is now threatened and so is the human population because humans depend almost entirely on the environment.

It is worth noting that there is more population increase in third world countries than developing countries. This difference in rates of population increase could be attributed to lack of policies to regulate population in African and other developing countries. Further, because of the uncontrolled birth rates, there is a rise in demand for many things some of them being food and shelter (Mishra, 2002). While the natural resources can easily provide us with what we want, it is important to note that we can only depend on natural environment but not for so long. The demand for food and shelter exerts pressure on agricultural land as there is need to construct more houses to cater for the rising populations. The effects of these populations on the environment are that they increase pollution, consumption of energy and also the depletion of arable land (Mishra, 2002). As it turns out, a continued increase in populations without a thought on how these populations would be sustained is suicidal. In what is termed as the ecological footprint, the population upsurge does not mean well for coming generations whereby there would be more than two billion people added on the current number of over seven billion.

A good example of the effects of uncontrolled population is Lesotho and Kenya which have been highly rated among the poor countries. In these two countries, there has been uncontrolled population growth which have ultimately led to sporadic shortages in food and almost prompted famines each year. The pressure being exerted on the environment by the upward trend in the population in these countries is becoming too much that the available natural resources cannot sustain. Further, because of uncontrolled birthrates there has also been encroachment of water catchment areas such as the Mau forest in Kenya which has been a sources of both the country's water and also a source of political animosity between those who want to conserve the environment and those who have been forced to look for new homes because of the population pressure in their areas.

In his hypothesis, Malthus related population increase to environmental degradation and thus cautioned the world on the need for checking population trends lest they end up without something to sustain them. However, Esther Boserup disputes this on the basis that when the population increases, there would be more pressure on governments to increase its agricultural production to cater for the rising demand for food for instance (Gould, 2015). The question worth asking is, where would these lands for agricultural expansion come from when an increase in population results into demand for housing?

In Somalia, another country in the developing world, there are more than five million people being affected with famine each year. For instance, according to a United Nations report in 2016, more people were at the threat of dying from hunger because of lack of food. This included over three hundred thousand children fifty thousand of which were totally suffering from malnutrition (Iyengar, 2016).Somalia is one of the countries professing the Muslim faith which allows men to marry as many as four women most of whom have more than three children each. This does not mean well for Somalia unless certain measures are put into place to address policies on population control.

Another case is Nigeria. Nigeria has the largest number of people in Africa. As such, it does not require a genius to figure out the implications of tens of millions of people in a country on the environment. The impact of Nigeria's population on environment has been worsening each year to the extent that congestion, soil depletion, climate change scarcity of food has become the order of the day (Theodore, 2006). While relating the scientific concept of matter occupying a limited space, Theodore (2006) argues that human beings (whom he refers to as matter) occupy a limited space (the environment). Further, he says that space is limited and the upsurge of Nigeria's population running into hundreds of millions would be disastrous if left unchecked.

HUMAN POPULATION

It is estimated that there is an annual increase in population by over ninety million people. This comes from the statistics from the year 2005 of about six and a half billion world population coupled with an annual growth rate of about 1.5%. In Nigeria alone, the population increase rates are already at over 2.5% (DPR Nigeria, 2005). Further, in Nigeria in a similar way as Somalia, there are quite many Muslims who are reported to encourage early marriages that have apparently contributed to the overwhelming rise in populations in the country. Theodore (2006) goes on relating the effects of population on pollution and climate change. For instance, high populations contributed to over twenty four million metric tons of carbon emissions in the year 2001. Compared to the rate of population increase stated above, one can easily conclude the impacts of such a population on the environment in the year 2017 and years to come (United Nation, 2011). Theodore concludes by crying for Nigeria as he does not see Nigeria being able to sustain its population in about twenty seven years' time. He notes that by then Nigeria could have reached its maximum carrying capacity and probably that's when the government would come to its senses but it would be too late to revert.

Secondly, most third world countries are still behind when it comes to many sectors. One of them is the agricultural sector which is still undergoing changes including embracing technologies among others. Consequently, the level of production seems to be lower than its levels of consumption. This has resulted in the increased importations of food products such as rice and maize. With this kind of production mess the third world countries are in, it does not support any forms of promotion of population growth. Some of these countries have been having problems feeding their growing populations in earlier years. What then could be their ability to feed their future populations which would be more compared to previous numbers coupled with unavailability of arable land among other factors of production? Definitely, the countries would be unable to cater for their rising populations.

Because of lack of creativity or regulation of their population growth rates, these countries which are still struggling with their agricultural sectors have failed to become innovative in terms of expanding their production. They have kept on relying on agriculture as the main source of livelihood and failed to take other issues such as controlling their population into concern. They have stuck on agriculture even when their arable land is being overwhelmed and depleted (Mittal & Mittal, 2013). Further, these countries characterized by massive rates of poverty have been ignorant of the need to control how they utile their natural resources by embarking on development projects that in turn come to harm the environment. While other countries in the developed world are busy researching on how to produce for instance environmentally friendly cars and products, these peasant countries are still struggling with social problems they could have averted had they put in place proper laws and policies. As such, it becomes a concern especially when populations increase yet the same means of sustaining themselves are being degraded (Mittal & Mittal, 2013). It follows therefore, that unless these countries concentrate on other means of production, they would end up depleting all their resources leaving their overwhelming populations to die in hunger and from effects of global warming among other factors that they could have avoided had they put in place the right policies on population control et al.

Third world countries have had clean environment and a lot of resources were still unexplored. This was so in the early nineteenth century but now things have drastically changed. With improved health developments in the world they can now be declared free of any diseases. This has in turn reduced mortality rates prompting an increase in population throughout the developing countries. Despite changes in world technology among other areas, poor countries have stuck to their old ways and instead of thinking of years to come, they keep on sleeping and thinking that all is well. Consequently, their populations have continued to increase thanks to medical advancements resulting into pressure on the environment. Resources have continued to be depleted by the increasing populations leading to climate and environmental concerns.

It is a good thing to have children and happy families. However, it would be disastrous to do this without thinking of how these people would be sustained. As it stands now, the resources that the world has are being depleted at alarming rates by the increase in human populations especially in developing countries. For instance, in the People's Republic of China, there are over two billion people. The amount of damage that this population has caused made on China is beyond description. The population has resulted into excessive demand for energy, food, shelter, social amenities, roads and transport facilities and this has resulted into nothing but degradation and continued depletion of natural resources (Mishra, 2002). As of now further, China has depleted most of its water sources, mineral deposits and the high demand for things like energy forces China to look for resources in third world states in Africa. This is just but a tip of the iceberg and unless other countries learn from China, the world resources most of which are still unexploited in Africa, would be depleted beyond recovery if population growth rates keep on going up unchecked. The impacts of uncontrolled birth rates would lead to further rising in global warming and continued melting of the icebergs meaning that the world may be soon submerged into water because of human activities.

Also, there are many threats to diseases associated with large populations (Gould, 2015). This is so especially because of the advancement in transport and communication systems worldwide which makes it very easy to traverse the world within short time. Therefore, because of large populations, it becomes hard to manage movements hence the ease of spreading infectious diseases. Further, it is hard to manage human behavior in highly populated countries leading to many health problems such as spread of HIV/AIDs and Ebola among others (Gould, 2015). To add on the preceding, human populations as mentioned earlier have the degrading effect on environment. Therefore, increased number of people means increase in depletion of natural resources which could in turn lead to exposure to harmful rays from the sun (Mittal & Mittal, 2013). For instance, exposure to harmful sun rays has been linked to the increasing cases of cancer patients worldwide.

A good instance is that that happened in Liberia and other West African countries a few years ago. One instance of Ebola infection spread so fast because of the congestion of people in the country. Consequently, it became hard to control the spread and it called for extreme measure including travel restrictions to ensure everyone stayed at their homesteads until the virus was contained.

With the foregoing in mind, it is important that governments in developing countries should take measures to control the increase in population. There is therefore a need to embark on a vigorous campaign to promote birth control in these developing countries because they are the main contributors to the surge in world populations (Mittal & Mittal, 2013). The fact that there are limited resources should guide mostly African countries in coming up with the best policies on not only birth regulation but also exploitation of the available resources.

Controlling human populations is essential in the sense that it would result in reduced consumption of natural resources; it would also result in controlled environmental pollution;

further, checking a country's population rates is essential in the sense that there would be enough time to prepare for any challenges be it health-wise or environmental (Mittal & Mittal, 2013). By controlling the number of people in a country, studies show that there would be an opportunity to make informed investment policies, there would also be an opportunity to manage and decide which areas to concentrate on unlike in a congested environment where it becomes hectic to control use of resources. Similarly, by controlling populations, it would be easier to give people the quality of life they deserve and also promote better living standards. Additionally, it would be easy to promote sustainable development resulting into long term benefits (Mittal & Mittal, 2013).

Another importance of controlling population growth lies in the protection of biodiversity. This is so because with a large number of people concentrated in one area, it becomes hard to control how they use certain natural resources such as water catchment areas. A controlled population would mean that there is a no pressure on natural resources unlike in a largely populous country. In the latter, the demand for resources would be high hence everyone would want to satisfy his or her needs without giving attention to what the future holds for them. Consequently, an unchecked population growth would be poisonous to the environment which is the only supplier of human needs and wants (Mittal & Mittal, 2013).

The human population issue should not be the problem of third world countries alone. Everyone needs to promote and advocate for the regulation of human population and this is necessary because the impacts of climate change do not affect a specific country but extend to other countries as well (Mittal & Mittal, 2013). When one country fails to regulate its population, the effects of huge populations such as emission of carbon into the environment and other forms of pollution, spread to the whole world thus threatening our existence as human beings and the other members of the ecosystem. There is need to develop policies that are alive to the fact that human population could be the biggest threat to the environment than any other factor (Mittal & Mittal, 2013). Also, it should be a requirement for every country to enact and implement policies that seek to regulate population. This should be collectively agreed upon between all countries in the world because population is a threat to the existence of the world itself.

The world is a fixed resource that if not well managed it could end up being dried up. Issues of population increase as such pose a great threat to the environment and there is urgent need move and tame the upward trend in world populations. It has been noted that most third world countries are responsible for population pressure on environment because they lack proper policies on birth control. Countries like Nigeria have kept on increasing in population despite the fact that there are limited resources available to cater for the increasing number of people. It has been established that religion could be one of the main reasons for population increase as for instance, Muslims encourage early marriages and polygamy and some religion such as Catholics have been publicly opposed to use of contraceptives. Further, the lack of goodwill from governments has also been contributing to population upsurge as these governments have been failing to pass laws and policies to regulate population. As such, it is important that third world countries especially, come up with measures to control how their resources would be used by controlling the number of children everyone should have (Filmer & Pritchett, 2002). Further, governments need to inform their people on the importance of controlling birth, as this would help people to participate in the move to save the world from climate change among other threats posed by rising number of human population.

In summary, human population increase has been linked to the environmental degradation that is currently being witnessed in most developing countries. Developing countries have failed to educate their people on the importance of birth control and this is being equated to cuddling a time bomb. Population upsurge greatly impacts negatively on the environment as the higher the population the more the pressure being exerted on the limited resources available. Additionally, it is important to know that while human population continues to grow, the resources to sustain their large numbers are gradually being depleted (Theodore, 2006).

These calls for all governments worldwide to exert pressure and impose sanctions if need be, on governments that fail to take the human population problem seriously. Uncontrolled births lead to increased populations hence increased pressure on the available resources. This means that there is dire need for policies to provide for the population problem before time runs out. Further, countries that still have no such policies should learn from the People's Republic of China as it is the best example of bad policies. China should teach other countries that the threat of population on environment is real. Every country needs to know that an increase in population results into increase in demand for food, shelter, energy among other human needs and thus, if not controlled, the biggest threat to human life is humans themselves. Humans have the ability to

HUMAN POPULATION

destroy an environment if not controlled. It therefore should be the function of governments to ensure that it does not leave room for any uncontrolled births.

HUMAN POPULATION

References

Filmer, D. & Pritchett, L. H. (2002). Environmental Degradation And The Demand For Children Searching For The Vicious Circle In Pakistan. Envinmental Division Econ. 2002;7;123-146

Gould, W.T.S., (2015). Population and development. Retrieved from https://books.google.co.ke/books?id=AsTlCAAAQBAJ&pg=PA19&lpg=PA19&dq=high+populations.and+diseases&source=bl&ots=dmWUZoiOj6&sig=hibDsFAhbmraZoYWINwdptwR7d4&hl=en&sa=Xved=ZahUKEwjzOJDHlfpXAhVFtBQKHWRkDDOQ6AEwBXoECAoQAA#v=onepage&q=high%20populations.and%20diseases&f=false Accessed on 4th December 2017.

Iyengar, R., (2016). Five Million People In Somalia Do Not Have food, The UN says. Retrieved from www.google.com/amp/amp.timeinc.net/time/4502298/somalia-food-shortage-un-famine-hunger Accessed on 4th December 2017.

Mishra, V., (2002). Population Growth and intensification of land use in India. Int J Popul Geogr. 2002;8:365-383

Mittal, R., & Mittal, C.G., (2013). Impact of population explosion on environment. The National Journal. Vol. 1. Issue 1. Pages 1-4

Theodore, I.O., (2006). The effects of population growth in Nigeria. Journal of applied Sciences,6: 1332-1337. Retrieved from http://scalert.net/abstract/?doi=jas.2006.1332.1337 Accessed on 4th December 2017.

United Nations Population Division (2011). World Population Prospects. The 2010 Revision. New York: UN Population Division.

YOUR KNOWLEDGE HAS VALUE

- We will publish your bachelor's and master's thesis, essays and papers

- Your own eBook and book - sold worldwide in all relevant shops

- Earn money with each sale

Upload your text at www.GRIN.com
and publish for free